A 15-minute Summary & Analysis

of

Marie Kondo's

The Life-Changing Magic of Tidying Up

By Instaread

Instaread on The Life-Changing Magic of Tidying Up by Marie Kondo

Please Note

This is an unofficial summary and analysis.

Copyright © 2014 by Instaread. All rights reserved worldwide. No part of this publication may be reproduced or transmitted in any form without the prior written consent of the publisher.

Limit of Liability/Disclaimer of Warranty: The publisher and author make no representations or warranties with respect to the accuracy or completeness of these contents and disclaim all warranties such as warranties of fitness for a particular purpose. The author or publisher is not liable for any damages whatsoever. The fact that an individual or organization is referred to in this document as a citation or source of information does not imply that the author or publisher endorses the information that the individual or organization provided. This concise summary is unofficial and is not authorized, approved, licensed, or endorsed by the original book's author or publisher.

Contents

SUMMARY 4

IMPORTANT PEOPLE 14

ANALYSIS 16

    Key Takeaway 1 18

    Key Takeaway 2 20

    Key Takeaway 3 23

    Key Takeaway 4 25

    Key Takeaway 5 27

    Key Takeaway 6 29

    Key Takeaway 7 31

    Key Takeaway 8 34

    Key Takeaway 9 36

    Key Takeaway 10 38

   Style Analysis 40

   Perspective 42

SUMMARY

Marie Kondo is a Japanese consultant specializing in tidying. In *The Life-Changing Magic of Tidying Up,* Kondo shares her simple method of tidying along with a wealth of insights into clutter, including what causes it and what types exist. Kondo also shares her own personal history and how that history led her to develop and refine her tidying method, referred to throughout the book as the KonMari Method.

People are not formally taught how to tidy, and many have difficulty learning as adults, resulting in homes that are cluttered. The KonMari Method substitutes for the class on tidying never offered at school that many could have benefited from.

Tidying has benefits that go beyond the pleasure a person takes in an ordered household. In fact, tidying can be life-changing as it gives a person skills that are transferrable to other life realms, such as occupation and relationships. The connection between mental health and the condition of a person's home is strong. As a person tidies, they learn more about their own mind and life.

The foundation of the KonMari Method is a thorough sorting of all items in the home, followed by discarding to reduce clutter, and concluding by choosing a place in the home for every item to be returned to. This one-time special event tidying is purposefully extreme so that it will shock and please a person so much that they will never return to their old clutter patterns. As Kondo puts it, "concentrate your efforts on eliminating clutter thoroughly and completely within a short span of time, you will see instant results that will empower you to keep your space in order ever after" (ch 1, EPUB).

Simplicity in all things is promoted throughout the book. Readers are advised to forgo mixing and matching with other methods, such as *feng shui*, flow planning, or tidying techniques tailored to different personality types. These are not necessary if one follows the KonMari Method. All people with tidying issues have either an inability to throw possessions out, an inability to put things back where they belong, or a combination of the two. Since there is not a complex set of causes, there is no need for a complex set of solutions.

On the psychological level, the human being who attracts clutter is often over-attached to the past or the future. The reluctance to let go of items because they might be needed someday is seen as coming out of anxiety about the future. Sentimental items are seen as clinging to the past. Both attachments must be overcome. A clean home environment allows a person to examine their state of mind, no longer distracted by the clutter around them. Ultimately, a tidying up gives a person the mental space to figure out what they truly want out of life. Many who have followed the method have gone on to change their lives in major ways.

Before beginning the process of discarding, a person should visualize their ideal apartment or home, asking themselves what they would like to see there. They should also ask themselves how they would like to feel in the home. It is not necessary to have a blueprint of how a person wants their home to end up, but the exercise will help prime them for the process of discarding, which hinges upon selecting which objects to keep and which to discard based on whether the object sparks joy. A visualization of the ideal apartment necessitates getting in touch with that feeling of joy.

A person starts tidying by gathering all items in one category in a central location. The best results occur in the early morning and when the environment is quiet. The categories of items to be sorted through are clothing first, second are books, third are papers, fourth is *komono* or small items, such as DVDs and beauty products, and fifth are sentimental items such as photographs and love letters.

The first move would be to gather all clothing from everywhere in the dwelling and put them in the same spot. Clothing also has a specific order of sorting. It should be gone through starting with tops, then moving to bottoms, clothes that should be hung, socks, underwear, bags, accessories, clothes for specific events, and finally, shoes.

The fundamental decision-making question should center around the question of whether the item causes a spark of joy. Joy is a quick feeling of unmistakable happiness upon handling the article. If it does not spark joy, discard it. There are several other tips about how to make the discarding process easy. A person should consider starting with off-season clothing that they feel less attached to. If a person is having trouble deciding, they might want to reframe their thinking so that they emphasize that they are choosing what to keep, not what to give away.

Next are books. A person should spread all books out on the floor of the chosen location. Again, a person should try to focus on books that cause a spark of joy. Eventually, a person should be able to pare their book collection down to their "Hall of Fame" books.

Now it is time for the third category, papers. The paper category does not include sentimental papers. A person should be left with only papers that need to be acted upon or kept permanently, like a birth certificate. Different classifications are mentioned in the book, such as warranties and lecture materials.

Sentimental items are saved for last because it is important to have honed a person's instinct for joy-sparking detection before tackling these long-treasured, but often dust-gathering, objects. It can be difficult for tidiers to imagine getting rid of cherished love letters, but keeping them only ensures that they are weighed down by their past.

In fact, letters of any kind fulfill their purpose the moment they are read. There is no real reason to keep them lying around. The letter writer has probably forgotten they mailed it and moved on. Photographs in particular become cumbersome in huge numbers, and a person must learn to sort the special photographs from the ones that are forgettable. In fact, too many pictures might make a trip or special occasion seem more boring and ordinary than it actually was.

If an object is broken or out of date, it should definitely be discarded. The joy-sparking question is the cornerstone of the KonMari Method and what makes it into a permanent solution. Once tidiers are surrounded only by objects that give them joy, they will learn to discard anything else automatically and never keep any object out of attachment to past or future again.

There are an assortment of helpful tips and insights sprinkled throughout the text about discarding. They include advice to keep family members away from the home while tidying, as they will often interfere and try to stop the tidier from getting rid of items. There are also anecdotes showing how adult children will often send things to their parents' home rather than getting rid of them, how younger siblings often end up with lots of hand-me-down clothes, and how a person should resist the urge to throw out family members' items.

A person will know when they are done discarding when their intuition tells them in a moment called the "just right click point." This moment differs from person to person and is entirely internal.

When the process of discarding is finished, it is time to learn how to store and take care of the items the tidier has chosen to keep. First and foremost, every item should have its place. Fancy storage units are for the most part worthless. Such units attract clutter and eventually overflow. Storage should not be complicated and should be centralized as much as possible.

Folded clothes, vertical storage, storing bags inside one another and the credo that "storage should reduce the effort needed to put things away" (ch. 4, EPUB), not to leave them out, are all things to keep in mind as a tidier goes about storing their joy-sparking possessions. It is important to remember to clip off all labels and unpack new items entirely before putting them away. A tidier should also avoid storing things near the tub or sink where they are bound to get messy.

Gratitude and appreciation of the inanimate is key. Eventually, the successful tidier must learn how to appreciate their belongings and offer thanks to them, even when discarding them. When the tidier comes to the stage of gratitude, they are probably experiencing some of the promised mental clarity. That mental clarity leads to better relationships and better job prospects. The tidier has zeroed in on what sparks joy in them and is a lot less likely to settle for less.

Tidying also makes a person more grateful for their dwelling. A person will find themselves listening more to their home. Without clutter, a person will be in harmony with their house or apartment, learning to appreciate it and also how to appropriately respond to its needs. Ultimately, a person "comes to know contentment" (ch. 5, EPUB) through tidying and lives a happier, more fulfilling life. The mental benefits of tidying are so manifold and obvious that the newly minted tidier will never fall back into their old ways again.

IMPORTANT PEOPLE

Marie Kondo: Marie Kondo, a tidying consultant, is the author of *The Life-Changing Magic of Tidying Up*. She frequently classifies her ideas and techniques under the umbrella term "the KonMari Method."

Marie Kondo's Sister: Kondo often gave her younger sister many hand-me-down clothes before realizing that, by doing so, she was making it harder for her sister to tidy correctly.

Marie Kondo's Family: Marie Kondo lived with her family for many years. Organizing and tidying their home greatly influenced her development as a tidying consultant.

A: A was a client who, rather than discard sentimental items, stored them in her parents' home, causing them a tidying problem

Client with Unhelpful Mother: This client attempted to discard items, but her mother took them, inhibiting her attempts to be tidy.

Client with Labels: This client was relatively tidy but felt something was off. Kondo discovered that she had too many items with labels still on them, creating mental clutter.

Client Who Went Into Childcare: After tidying up her books, this client discovered her true passion did not lie in a corporate job but in childcare, so she started her own business.

Client with Brown Jacket: This client completed a course presented by Kondo, but Kondo went through her drawers and uncovered a brown jacket that she intuitively knew brought the client no joy.

Nagisa Tasumi: Tasumi is the author of *The Art of Discarding*, a book that had a profound impact on Kondo.

Instaread on The Life-Changing Magic of Tidying Up by Marie Kondo

ANALYSIS

Key Takeaways & Analysis of Key Takeaways

Key Takeaway 1

Tidying is something everyone should know how to do. Kondo's tidying method is one-size fits all.

Analysis

Early in the book, the idea that personality type or personal history dictates what techniques a person should adopt when tidying is dismissed. The KonMari Method of tidying is universal.

The book uses the term tidying, which may provoke confusion, because tidying can be associated with a light ordering of a living space and its possessions. The way the book uses tidying is closer to the American term of decluttering. The scope of the book extends beyond decluttering in that advice is given on how to store remaining possessions. While the word choice might initially disorient some readers, the general topic will be familiar to an American public that has already been exposed to the concept of minimalism when it comes to keeping the home.

Kondo offers no hard evidence in the form of surveys or focus groups that the KonMari Method works universally, and some readers might be resistant to the idea that there is a one-size-fits-all solution. They could point to the fact that almost all of the book's anecdotes feature female professionals in their thirties. For some readers, about what to do with this cohort's possessions, such as high heel shoes and makeup, might not seem helpful at first glance to a teen male wondering what to do with his video games. However, a reader is meant to ignore such details and stick to the general lessons imparted that should be capable of being applied to a wide variety of clutter.

Key Takeaway 2

Tidying is a special event that should occur one-time only and the effects will be permanent.

Analysis

The idea that a one-time, single event is needed to induce significant change in a person's life will be welcome to readers who face a barrage of tidying tips coming at them from popular magazines such as *Woman's World* and *O* as well as on TV networks such as Home and Garden Television and Style Network. First, such a vast, unending march of tips implicitly supports the idea that tidying is a lifetime job. Second, many of the tips themselves explicitly contain ongoing directives, such as "clean the kitchen every Monday".

Kondo's claims are reminiscent of those implied by the cable television show *Hoarders*. On *Hoarders*, a team of experts assists a person who hoards items by doing a one-time, special event clean-out.[1] For most of the show's broadcast, only the special event has been shown, not life after the dehoarding. The viewer did not know if the hoarder becomes naturally tidy forevermore until follow-up episodes. Recently, a series of Where Are They Now? episodes have shown that there have been a mixed bag of results when it comes to maintaining the clean conditions.[2] Some reverted to their hoarder ways.

There are some differences between the show and Kondo's book. A person could argue that hoarders have a mental condition and should not be compared to those with some clutter. Another difference between the show's hoarders and those who buy Kondo's book is that the book buyers have been inspired to tidy on their own. Most of

---

[1] Rose, Tracy, "'Hoarders' Update on Lifetime Could Revive Show,"*Guardian Liberty Voice*, accessed December 18, 2014,
http://guardianlv.com/2014/05/hoarders-update-on-lifetime-could-revive-show/

[2] Rose, Tracy, "'Hoarders' Update on Lifetime Could Revive Show,"*Guardian Liberty Voice*, accessed December 18, 2014,
http://guardianlv.com/2014/05/hoarders-update-on-lifetime-could-revive-show/

the hoarders have been urged to change their ways by relatives. So, just because there have been mixed results on the show while Kondo says she has a one hundred percent success rate does not mean that Kondo is misrepresenting her method.

The duration of the special event tidying will naturally vary according to how much clutter each individual has. It might seem to take significantly more time than other systems or techniques, but it will allow the tidier to see much more dramatic results faster, and that will inspire him or her.

Key Takeaway 3

Family is often an impediment to tidying. They, as well as their possessions, should be largely ignored while tidying.

Analysis

Kondo suggests that beginner tidiers focus on their own possessions since tidying up family possessions can have negative consequences. The often owners get upset their objects have been moved or discarded. Furthermore, while preparing to discard a person's own possessions, family can often disrupt the process by attaching sentimental value to items and preventing the discarding from occurring.

Since so much of the book is geared toward people freeing themselves, first from possessions, and then from whatever other constraints they feel are placed on their lives, it stands to reason that family with its emotional bonds and long history that, while often loving and happy, can tug and confine the individual, should be kept out of the process. To witness the drama inherent in every family, no matter how loving, a person need to look no further than any popular reality show centered on families.

Kondo's suggestion that family members are more likely to change their own attitudes toward clutter after they see a family member's change also resonates with the common admonition to be the change a person wants to see, often attributed to Mahatma Gandhi. Gandhi's original quote was far longer, but the essential meaning is caught by the shorter sentence. Ghandi personified being the change and attracted many followers. These were people who adopted his principles without having to be browbeaten to do so. A person can hope that untidy family members, seeing the example of a tidy person, will make change on their own without having to be nagged about it.

Key Takeaway 4

There are two main steps to tidying. First, discarding extraneous objects and second, putting everything back in a defined place.

Analysis

The simplicity of Kondo's plan is undeniable. On that basis alone, many will be drawn to it, already fatigued from dealing with complex work and social lives. No one wants taking care of their home to become like a second job, which might happen if a person has to pick up a decluttering book with many steps.

The merits of the first step, discarding, is easy to understand, especially since the economic downturn has caused Americans to shift their focus from accumulating possessions to accumulating experiences.

Although Kondo is convincing about the value of discarding, there is not nearly as much information about figuring out where to put everything that remains. Perhaps this is because she has not seen as much difficulty in the finding a place for the remaining items in her consulting business as she has with the discarding. It could also be that it is easier to make blanket statements about possessions than about people's living spaces, which vary tremendously. The book cannot be too specific about where to put things when layouts are so different.

Key Takeaway 5

Discarding is a very intuitive process that must be honed and refined. When choosing what to discard, a person must consider whether an object sparks joy.

Analysis

The book discusses what goes into discarding in-depth. The KonMari Method rejects traditional criteria, like discarding clothing a person has not worn in a year in favor of something more abstract. Kondo urges people to discard based on whether an item sparks joy.

Discarding based on joy-sparking is unique to this book. Kondo originated the concept of joy sparking and spends a fair amount of pages elucidating it. It is not as Bohemian as a person might at first glance think and will resonate with readers who have explored the idea of intuition or instinct based decision making before. The notion that important decisions can be made very quickly was fully and popularly explored in Malcolm Gladwell's *Blink*. For readers of New Age and self-help books, this concept will also be familiar as such books suggest that a person be in touch with their inner spirit and make decisions based on intuition or gut instinct.

On the other hand, logic-oriented people might have trouble accepting the joy-sparking criteria, or not fully understand it. Without accepting this central premise, the reader might find themselves stymied in following Kondo's advice, as it is clear that Kondo feels this is the only way to have effective tidying. Luckily, the book promises that understanding is not necessary and that a person can learn experientially what it feels to have an object spark joy.

Key Takeaway 6

Storage solutions should not be overly complicated, or they lead to more clutter. As long as possessions have been sorted and everything has its own place, complex storage systems are unnecessary.

Analysis

Kondo has personally tried out complex storage systems, either ones that can be crafted at home or ones she bought at stores. The book challenges the idea that these storage systems are truly helpful and instead suggests that once a thorough tidying occurs, there will be no need for complicated storage spaces.

Her message may be enticing to readers who have bought many such systems only to find that their space remains untidy. Stores like *The Container Store* are built around saving people space, and their products can end up taking a lot out of people's wallets without giving them much return. The use of sophisticated storage systems brings to mind the adage about treating the symptoms but not the disease. The symptom is the clutter, but the disease is being unable or reluctant to discard items that do not spark joy.

Kondo's directive that everything should have its own place will resonate with those familiar with the French idea of *mise en place*, which stems from cuisine and refers to how all ingredients and tools necessary to create a meal should be set up in advance of cooking, each in its own place. In a place like a kitchen, disorder can create chaos, leading to inferior work. While the clutter at home perhaps has less visible consequences, it leads someone to feel unhappy inside.

Key Takeaway 7

Belongings should be treasured, thanked, and treated with care. Belongings want to be used, and if they are not wanted or used, they want to be let go.

Analysis

Belongings are personified throughout the book. Again, this might strike more logic oriented readers as unnecessary, but a person does not have to believe that belongings are sentient beings to garner something worthwhile from the idea that they should be treated as such.

If a person treats their belongings as if they are conscious, they will be more inclined to treat them better. When a person finds themselves in a situation where professional tidying services are needed, or a tidying book is required, it is likely that their belongings are not being treated with care. They are being squeezed and piled upon, creating general disorder and likely damaging them. If a person thanked them and appreciated their worth, it is likely that they would treat them better.

The book comes together with current zeitgeist about the power of gratitude. Gratitude journals have become popular. Oprah Winfrey often mentions hers.[3] Gratitude is seen as a character trait that, if developed, leads to a better, more positive life. For this reason, it will be easy for readers to connect thanking items to positive changes in their own lives.

Another way Kondo personifies belongings is when she asserts that if they are not used, or do not spark joy, they want to be let go. This speaks powerfully to the reader who might feel guilty for discarding objects, almost as if they were killing

---

[3] Winfrey, Oprah, "What Oprah Knows for Sure About Gratitude," Oprah.com, accessed December 18, 2014, http://www.oprah.com/spirit/Oprahs-Gratitude-Journal-Oprah-on-Gratitude

them, or at least letting them, and the memory they carry, down.

Key Takeaway 8

Problems with discarding come down to attachment to the past or anxiety about the future.

Analysis

Kondo found that if a client has decided that a possession does not spark joy but is still having trouble discarding it, the problem usually comes down to their being too attached to the past or worried about the future.

Clients can learn a lot about themselves through these thought patterns about objects. Kondo's insights here verge into psychology. It is accepted that anxiety about the future greatly affects people and can lead them to make poor life decisions, not to mention having negative effects on health.[4]

---

[4] "How Worrying Affects the Body," Web MD, last accessed December 18, 2014 http://www.webmd.com/balance/guide/how-

Objects from the past often bring up shame, they can represent poor decisions, such as love letters from a romance that turned sour for example. Clutter therefore becomes something that can allow a person to see in concrete terms how much anxiety or attachment to the past is affecting them. This may be as effective as talk therapy in getting people to change their behavior.

The discussion of how tidying relates to the past and future as well as people's feelings about them is almost therapeutic and its lessons are easily transferrable to realms outside of tidying. Relationships and jobs are often maintained in a person's life for the same reasons as clothes that no longer are worn.

Key Takeaway 9

Tidying, when done right, is done by category rather than location.

Analysis

Rather than approach tidying on a room-by-room basis, the book promotes the idea that clients should sort by category. Since similar items are stored in different places, going room by room will proceed too slowly. If a person tackles the clothes in one bedroom and then starts doing books, when they find books and clothes in another area, it will take time to get back in the groove sorting as they struggle to remember the standards for judging clothes and books. It is also possible that going room by room also takes away the shock value of seeing the full volume of how much of one item a person has. The shock value is a crucial motivator to discard.

A quick reading of this book might lead a person to boil it down to throw out almost everything owned, but it is important to pay attention to subtle points such as sort by category, not by location. To the eye that has not ever received an education in tidying, there might not be much of a difference between going room by room versus going by category. After all, when shown a house, people tend to go room by room. However, Kondo's alternative method of tackling the tidying makes sense, especially since she thoroughly explains her reasoning behind it.

Key Takeaway 10

Tidying, when done right, will initiate the start of a brand new life. The skills earned through tidying are applicable to many other areas in life. This is the magic of tidying.

Analysis

Amazing changes could be in store once people follow the KonMari Method. Tidying can lead to finding the right career path or the right relationship. When people have gotten used to seeing the effects of surrounding themselves only by possessions that spark joy, they begin to seek the same in their outside lives, discarding what they feel they need to keep out of obligation.

Though the word magic is used, some of the changes seem surprisingly grounded and similar to the logical conclusion of the kind of tidying the book promotes. For example, the worker who realizes that only books about social welfare spark joy in her, switches to a career in childcare. It is not just magic, the worker had already chosen to buy those books, tidying just led her to recognize the significance of them.

Decision-making is also improved, since tidiers have decided whether to keep or toss so many items. It is also claimed that tidying helps weight loss. These promises are appealing, but the only evidence given is from Kondo's experiences with her own clientele and her own logic. Some readers may be skeptical without some sort of scientific trial. Their skepticism could be heightened by some of Kondo's advice, such as to talk to possessions and to greet houses.

Style Analysis

The Life-Changing Magic of Tidying Up is a fairly short book, comprised of five chapters broken into smaller sections of varied numbers per chapter. All the chapters and sections have sentence long titles. The book is arranged chronologically to accompany a reader through their tidying journey.

Kondo writes with vigor and a clear sense of purpose. Readers sense that her writing style reflects her tidying style, intuitive and flowing prioritized over a rigid structure. Kondo takes care to make sure the book is lean and mean rather than bloated with extraneous verbiage. There are some Japanese terms scattered throughout, but all are explained thoroughly. Numerous client anecdotes keep the book feeling lively. For a small book, there is a fair amount of repetition, but readers have the sense that this is done because Kondo feels these points need to be repeated until they sink in. Perhaps she has worked with many recalcitrant clients.

Perspective

Kondo writes about her techniques with great confidence. Most of what she has learned has come from her own history of trying out, and failing, many techniques, programs, and storage solutions or from intuitive leaps she has made from observing her clients. Readers who need to be convinced by strong arguments might remain skeptical, particularly at some of the more New-Age infused advice and promises, but Kondo comes across as completely sincere, and her advice is detailed and practical enough to seem worth giving a try.

~~~~~~ END OF SUMMARY~~~~~~~

Made in the USA
Charleston, SC
19 March 2015